States

WASHINGTON, D.C.

by Bridget Parker

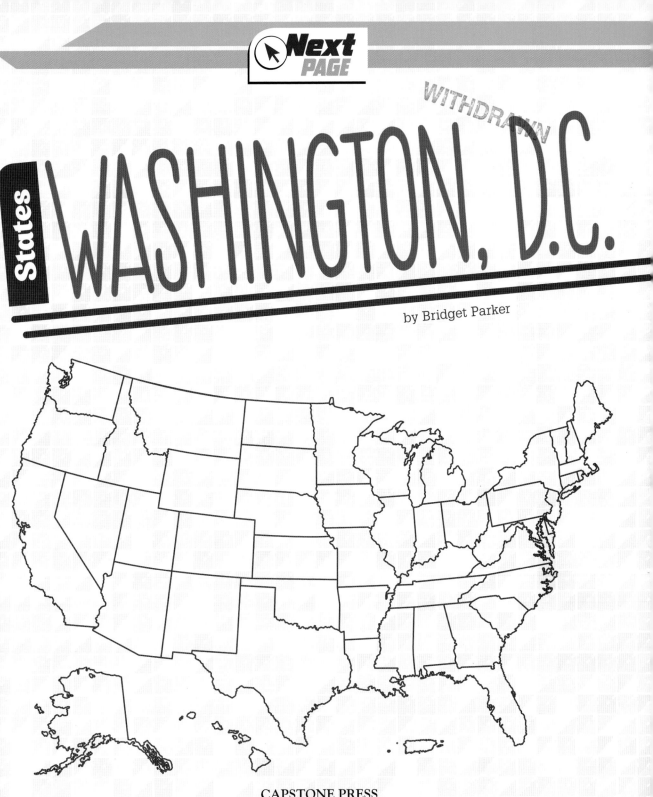

CAPSTONE PRESS
a capstone imprint

Next Page Books are published by Capstone Press,
1710 Roe Crest Drive, North Mankato, Minnesota 56003
www.mycapstone.com

Library of Congress Cataloging-in-Publication Data
Cataloging-in-publication information is on file with the Library of
Congress.
ISBN 978-1-5157-0436-2 (library binding)
ISBN 978-1-5157-0495-9 (paperback)
ISBN 978-1-5157-0547-5 (ebook PDF)

Editorial Credits
Jaclyn Jaycox, editor; Richard Korab and Katy LaVigne, designers;
Morgan Walters, media researcher; Tori Abraham, production specialist

Photo Credits
Capstone Press: Angi Gahler, map 4, 7; Getty Images: Michael Ochs
Archives, top 18; Newscom: Everett Collection, middle 18; One Mile
Up, Inc., flag, seal 23; Shutterstock: Andrea Izzotti, 16, Chris Hill, 21,
Cvandyke, 9, dibrova, 15, EastVillage Images, cover, Everett Historical,
12, 25, 26, 27, Featureflash, middle 19, fstockfoto, 5, Guillermo
Olaizola, 17, Helga Esteb, bottom 18, Jorg Hackemann, 29, Lissandra
Melo, 13, 14, M DOGAN, 6, 28, Olga Bogatyrenko, bottom 24, Orhan
Cam, 7, bottom left 8, 11, photo.ua, 10, Rena Schild, top 24, s_bukley,
top 19, bottom 19, Songquan Deng, bottom right 8; Wikimedia: Anders
Lagerås, top 20, HomeinSalem, bottom 20

All design elements by Shutterstock

Printed and bound in China.
0316/CA21600187
012016 009436F16

TABLE OF CONTENTS

Want to take your research further? Ask your librarian if your school subscribes to PebbleGo Next. If so, when you see this helpful symbol 🖱 throughout the book, log onto www.pebblegonext.com for bonus downloads and information.

LOCATION

Washington, D.C., is in the northeastern United States. It is not part of any state. Maryland borders it on the north, east, and south. Virginia lies to the south and west across the Potomac River. The District of Columbia was made up of three cities when it was built. Washington City, Georgetown, and Alexandria were all inside the district's borders. Over time, the three cities grew into one large city. Now all of the District of Columbia is called Washington, D.C. The federal government and an elected city council run the city.

PebbleGo Next Bonus!
To print and label your own map, go to www.pebblegonext.com and search keywords:
DC MAP

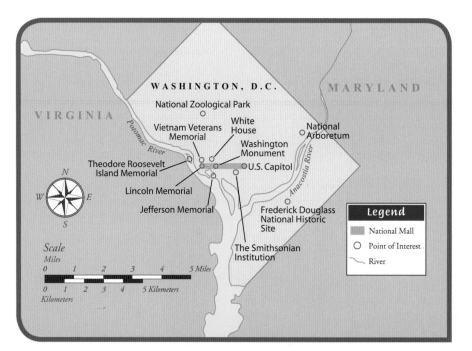

WASHINGTON, D.C.

MARYLAND

VIRGINIA

National Zoological Park

White House

Vietnam Veterans Memorial

National Arboretum

Potomac River

Washington Monument

Theodore Roosevelt Island Memorial

U.S. Capitol

Anacostia River

Lincoln Memorial

Jefferson Memorial

Frederick Douglass National Historic Site

The Smithsonian Institution

N
W   E
S

Scale
Miles
0   1   2   3   4   5 Miles

0   1   2   3   4   5 Kilometers
Kilometers

Legend
▨ National Mall
○ Point of Interest
⌁ River

Washington, D.C., covers 68 square miles (176 square kilometers) and is home to nearly 650,000 people.

GEOGRAPHY

Washington, D.C., was built on the marshlands and plains around the Potomac River. Some areas along the Potomac are only about 12 inches (30 centimeters) above sea level. The western edge of Washington, D.C., lies along the base of the Appalachian Mountains. The highest point in the District of Columbia is the historic Tenleytown neighborhood at 410 feet (125 meters) above sea level.

PebbleGo Next Bonus! To watch a video about the Lincoln Memorial and the Vietnam Veterans Memorial, go to www.pebblegonext.com and search keywords:

DC VIDEO

The Potomac River creates part of the western and southern borders of the District of Columbia.

The Jefferson Memorial, located on the Tidal Basin, was inspired by the Pantheon in Rome.

Legend

▲ Highest Point

▢ Park

〰 River

PIEDMONT PLATEAU

Tenleytown ▲

ROCK CREEK PARK

Potomac River

Rock Creek

Theodore Roosevelt Island

Anacostia River

ATLANTIC COASTAL PLAIN

Scale

Miles
0 1 2 3 4 5 Miles

0 1 2 3 4 5 Kilometers
Kilometers

N W E S

WEATHER

Washington, D.C., summers are warm. Winters are usually mild. The average winter temperature is 34 degrees Fahrenheit (1 degree Celsius). The average summer temperature is 74°F (23°C). The Atlantic Ocean keeps the air in the city humid during the summer.

Average High and Low Temperatures (Washington, D.C.)

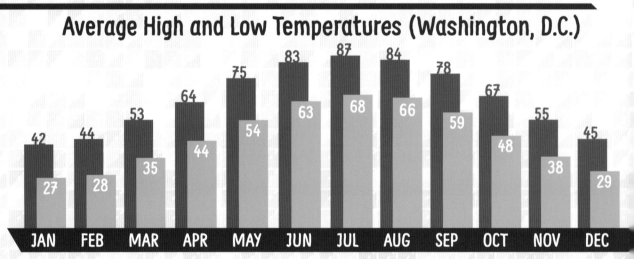

	JAN	FEB	MAR	APR	MAY	JUN	JUL	AUG	SEP	OCT	NOV	DEC
High	42	44	53	64	75	83	87	84	78	67	55	45
Low	27	28	35	44	54	63	68	66	59	48	38	29

LANDMARKS

National Mall

This strip of land contains most of the famous landmarks and important government buildings in the nation's capital. The Washington Monument, the Lincoln Memorial, the White House, the Capitol, and several war memorials are all located on the Mall. Millions of people visit these places each year.

Smithsonian

The Smithsonian Institution is the world's largest museum. Founded in 1846, it consists of 19 museums and galleries. The Smithsonian's museums hold dinosaur fossils, NASA spacecraft, and famous works of art.

Rock Creek Park

Rock Creek Park is one of the most beautiful nature spots in Washington, D.C. People enjoy hiking, biking, picnicking, bird watching, and jogging at the park.

The British army set fire to the Capitol on August 24, 1814, in the War of 1812.

The country's first capital was in Philadelphia, Pennsylvania. Many other cities wanted to be the capital. Congress decided a new capital city needed to be built. In 1791 President George Washington chose an area along the Potomac River. The new capital district was carved out of Maryland and Virginia. John Adams, the second president, and other politicians agreed to honor Washington by naming the main city in the district Washington City. Congress and President Adams moved to the new capital in 1800. In 1893 Congress extended the city of Washington into the rest of the District of Columbia.

Congress controls part of the budget of Washington, D.C., but the city elects its own leaders. The mayor leads the executive branch. The city council, with 13 members, is Washington's legislative branch. The District of Columbia Court of Appeals leads the judicial branch.

The Capitol has 540 rooms. Paintings and sculptures conveying American history are found throughout the building.

INDUSTRY

Washington, D.C., is not large enough to support the industries that support other states. Washington's economy is based on government, service industries, and tourism. Many people work for the U.S. government in Washington. All of the politicians in Washington have staff members who work for them. Lawyers, policy advisors, speechwriters, secretaries, and personal assistants work at the White House. The U.S. military has many people working in Washington, D.C.

Almost 4 million people visit the Lincoln Memorial each year.

Think tanks are one of Washington's unique businesses. A think tank is a business that finds solutions to difficult problems.

More than 19 million tourists visit the city each year. Tourists visit the U.S. Capitol, the Lincoln Memorial, the Washington Monument, and the Smithsonian Institution along a strip of land called the National Mall.

The Washington Monument was built to honor America's first president, George Washington.

POPULATION

Washington, D.C., was built to represent the people of the United States. The city reflects much of the nation's diversity. People of many races and cultures live in and visit the city. In recent years Washington's population has increased. Crime rates have fallen. More people are moving to the city to buy homes, rent office space, and start businesses. Since its early days, Washington has had a large African-American population. Today about half of Washington's citizens are African-American.

Population by Ethnicity

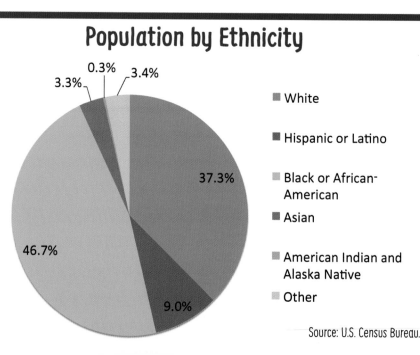

- White
- Hispanic or Latino
- Black or African-American
- Asian
- American Indian and Alaska Native
- Other

0.3%
3.4%
3.3%
37.3%
46.7%
9.0%

Source: U.S. Census Bureau.

Rolling Thunder is an annual motorcycle rally held in Washington, D.C. It's a tribute to American war heroes. The event draws nearly one million people from all over the country.

FAMOUS PEOPLE

Duke Ellington (1899–1974) was a jazz pianist and composer. Some of his best-known tunes are "Mood Indigo" and "Sophisticated Lady." His real name was Edward Kennedy Ellington. He was born in Washington, D.C.

John Philip Sousa (1854–1932) was a composer and band leader. He wrote more than 100 pieces for marching bands, including "The Stars and Stripes Forever" and "The Washington Post March."

Stephen Colbert (1964–) is a comedian and hosts a TV talk show. He was born in Washington, D.C.

Bill Nye (1955–) grew up in Washington, D.C. He hosted the TV show *Bill Nye the Science Guy*. He works as a scientist and promotes science education.

Samuel L. Jackson (1948–) is an actor. He has starred in many movies, including some of the *Star Wars* movies and *Unbreakable*. He was born in Washington, D.C.

Andrew Luck (1989–) is a professional NFL quarterback for the Indianapolis Colts. He was born in Washington, D.C.

DISTRICT SYMBOLS

scarlet oak

American beauty rose

Bird

wood thrush

PebbleGo Next Bonus! To make a dessert honoring past president Thomas Jefferson go to www.pebblegonext.com and search keywords:
DC RECIPE

FAST FACTS

DATE CITY BECOMES NATION'S CAPITAL
1800

SIZE
61 square miles (158 square kilometers)
land area (2010 U.S. Census Bureau)

POPULATION
646,449 (2013 U.S. Census estimate)

DISTRICT NICKNAME
The Nation's Capital

DISTRICT MOTTO
"Justitia Omnibus," which means "Justice for All" in Latin

OFFICIAL SEAL

Washington, D.C., adopted its official seal in 1871. The seal shows a woman placing a wreath on George Washington's statue. The woman represents justice. A bald eagle, the national bird, sits next to the woman. The U.S. Capitol is seen behind her. A ribbon with the city's motto is at the bottom of the seal. "Justitia Omnibus" means "Justice for All" in Latin.

PebbleGo Next Bonus!
To print and color your own flag, go to www.pebblegonext.com and search keywords:

DC FLAG

DISTRICT FLAG

Washington, D.C., adopted the district flag in 1938. It shows three red stars and two red bars on a white background. The flag is based on the shield of George Washington's coat of arms.

PROFESSIONAL SPORTS TEAMS

Washington Redskins (NFL)

Washington Nationals (MLB)

Washington Wizards (NBA)

Washington Mystics (WNBA)

Washington Capitals (NHL)

D.C. United (MLS)

PebbleGo Next Bonus! To learn the lyrics to the state song, go to www.pebblegonext.com and search keywords:

DC SONG

WASHINGTON, D.C. TIMELINE

1600s Nacostin, Anacostine, and Susquehannok American Indian tribes live in the Washington, D.C., area.

1620 The Pilgrims establish a colony in the New World in present-day Massachusetts.

1620s Leonard Calvert leads settlers into Maryland.

1783 American colonists win the Revolutionary War (1775–1783) against Great Britain and win their freedom.

1791 George Washington selects the location for the country's new capital city.

 1800 President Adams and Congress move to Washington, D.C.; Congress first meets in the new capital on November 17.

 **1814** On August 24 the president's house, officially known at the time as the Executive Mansion, is burned by British troops during the War of 1812 (1812–1815).

1862 On April 16 President Abraham Lincoln abolishes slavery in Washington, D.C.

**1861–1865** The Union and the Confederacy fight the Civil War. As the capital of the Union and resting on the border with the Confederacy, Washington, D.C., becomes the most heavily defended city in North America.

**1865** President Lincoln is assassinated at Ford's Theatre on April 14.

1884 The Washington Monument is completed.

1893 Congress passes a law extending the city of Washington into the rest of the District of Columbia.

**1901** President Theodore Roosevelt officially gives the White House its current name.

1922 The Lincoln Memorial is completed.

1932 World War I veterans come to Washington, D.C., to protest for "bonus pay" for time served in the war.

1943 The Jefferson Memorial is completed.

1961 District of Columbia residents gain the right to vote for the president.

1963 Dr. Martin Luther King Jr. makes his "I Have a Dream" speech in Washington, D.C., on August 28.

 **1974** Washington, D.C., elects its first mayor on November 5.

 **1982** The Vietnam Veterans Memorial is dedicated.

 **1993** The U.S. Holocaust Memorial Museum opens.

 2011 On August 23 an earthquake in Virginia damages buildings in Washington, D.C.

 2015 The Cuban embassy is reopened in Washington, D.C., 54 years after the United States broke diplomatic ties with the country.

Glossary

abolish *(uh-BOL-ish)*—to put an end to something officially

budget *(BUHJ-it)*—a plan for how money will be earned and spent

executive *(ig-ZE-kyuh-tiv)*—the branch of government that makes sure laws are followed

fossil *(FOSS-uhl)*—the remains or traces of an animal or a plant from millions of years ago, preserved as rock

gallery *(GAL-uh-ree)*—a place where art is shown and sold

industry *(IN-duh-stree)*—a business which produces a product or provides a service

legislature *(LEJ-iss-lay-chur)*—a group of elected officials who have the power to make or change laws for a country or state

marshland *(MARSH-land)*—an area of wet, low land

memorial *(muh-MOR-ee-uhl)*—something that is built or done to help people continue to remember a person or an event

Pilgrim *(PIL-gruhm)*—one of the English Separatists or other colonists who settled in North America in 1620

politician *(pol-uh-TISH-uhn)*—someone who runs for or holds a government office

Read More

Ganeri, Anita. *United States of America: A Benjamin Blog and His Inquisitive Dog Guide.* Country Guides. Chicago: Heinemann Raintree, 2015.

Hicks, Terry Allan. *Washington, D.C.* It's My State! New York: Cavendish Square Publishing, 2014.

Hirsch, Rebecca E. *What's Great About Washington, D.C.?* Our Great States. Minneapolis: Lerner Publications, 2015.

Internet Sites

FactHound offers a safe, fun way to find Internet sites related to this book. All of the sites on FactHound have been researched by our staff.

Here's all you do:

Visit *www.facthound.com*

Type in this code: 9781515704362

 Check out projects, games and lots more at
www.capstonekids.com

Critical Thinking Using the Common Core

1. How many professional sports teams does Washington, D.C., have? Name two. (Key Ideas and Details)

2. According to the timeline, how many years after Washington, D.C., became the capital did Congress first meet there? (Craft and Structure)

3. What three cities made up the District of Columbia when it was built? (Key Ideas and Details)

Index